Misty Morning
By
Earl Thompson

Misty Morning
EARL THOMPSON
COPYRIGHT 2012 EARL THOMPSON
FIRST EDITION
ISBN 9781105-88168-8
Publisher: Lulu.com

ACKNOWLEDGEMENT

Thanks to Judith Scott – Robinson for giving me the title of
the book and for inspiring the titled poem.

MISTY MORNING

Oh, misty morning, are you missing the sunshine too?
I guess you feel as sad and as lonely as I do?
I always feel sad whenever the sunshine stays away
because it always seems like only gloom will fill my day
I loathe the lazy days that you seem to bring
Because it always makes me feel drained, not wanting to do
a thing
During the winter that's the time you mostly appear
And you darken my days as if you don't care
In the summer, you sometime show yourself too
And that's when I feel sad, lonely and blue
Misty morning, I hope you can see
That all you bring to me is misery
The next time you go, please stay
And I promise I'll be thankful to you, until my dying day

THE THOUGHT OF YOU

I know that our love can never be
But the thought of you is an inspiration to me
I know that we shall forever be apart
But the thought of you does wonders to my heart
Whenever I'm feeling down
The thought of you helps me to come around
The thought of you helps me with my chores
It helps my down trodden spirit to soar
The thought of you is something I can't seem to do without
Because it's inspiring to me without a doubt
Holding you in my thoughts is what helps me to thrive
Sometimes it's the only thing that keeps me alive
When my days are cold and blue
The thought of you is what pulls me through
The thought of you helps to brighten my day
So that I can see the light in a very special way

A Message Of Condolence

I know it's hard when you lose someone you love
But there is someone who cares, the creator above
In times like these, you'll want to brood over the situation,
But what it calls for is for you to be brave and strong.
When you lose someone you love, it's like the world for
you ends
But there are people around you, people who are your
friends
Life must go on, though hard it may seems
You've got it ahead of you, your hopes and your dream
We all know that in the midst of life there is death
But you can't just sit around and fret
you'll have to be brave and strong
Because the creator is waiting to help you along.

A WOMAN FOR ALL TIMES

She has a heart of gold no one can see
She is a woman, beautiful and carefree
She is the woman any man would want in his life
She is the perfect example of a wife
She is never in the company of idle girls
She is always doing something positive to better her world
Her life has never always been the best
And she has been through some very rigorous tests
But she has never allowed the negatives to get her down
a woman of strength and character; she never wears a
frown
She can be approached by anyone, and always wears a
smile
She can lighten your burden if you stop and talk to her a
while
She can empathize with anyone because she has been there
too
Her dreams have been shattered, her heart broken in two
She has been called names she dare not mention
But they have only made her stronger, made her a better
woman
She is not angry with the world as you can see
She is enjoying Mother Nature, and all of her creativities
though the world is treating her as if she has committed a
crime
She is not angry, because she is a woman for all times.

HAVE FAITH IN ME

Loving you is like a dream come true
And for the rest of my life that is what I want to do
I don't know how it came to be
That of all the men in the world, you came to me
I was alone with no one in the world
And then you came and became my girl
You are everything I ever wanted in a woman
And for you I'll be the best that I can
You don't have to fear that I might leave and go away
Because for the rest of my life, beside you is where I want
to stay
All I ask is that you have faith in me
And we'll have the best future there can ever be

I Miss You

When you feel the way that I do
Then you will know what I am going through
Since you have been gone, life hasn't been the same
And I go to bed at nights and wake up calling your name
Every time I close my eyes, I see your face
And I get the feeling you're in a terrible place
Is he taking care of you the way I used to do?
Or is he hurting and torturing you?
Are you thinking of coming back to me?
Or are you living in captivity
On your face, do you still have that beautiful smile?
Or because of him have you changed your style?
I so badly need to hear from you
That I am just sitting here not knowing what to do
I keep looking at the phone and hoping for it to ring
But it's like I am deaf; I can't hear a thing
Please call me; I'm hoping to hear you're all right
So that I can go back to sleeping at nights
I miss you

<u>I remember Jamaica</u>
I remember Jamaica, a land full of golden sunlight
I remember Jamaica, a land so warm and bright
I remember walking by the sea
with the warm wind blowing in my face, mesmerizing me
I remember when I couldn't wait to see another day
because it would take the stress and heartache away
Jamaica, I yearn for your warm embrace
I long to feel the warmth of your sunlight, caressing my
face
I yearn to see the beautiful days you bring
I'm longing to see the Humming birds, speedily flopping
their wings
I long to feel your warm sunlight reaching to my very
bones
because this cold is making me feel so all alone
I remember Jamaica, where the grass is green all year
around
and there is never ever, any snow on the ground
I remember Jamaica with a beauty so extreme
with its rivers, ponds and delightful streams
Jamaica, a land that makes one feel so young and free
Jamaica, my land of liberty.

IF YOU WERE MINE

If I had the world, I'd give it to you
I'd give you everything you want;
I'd make your dreams come true
You'd be as happy as can be
Because you would be all that matter to me
There would be no tear for you to cry
But if you do, I'd be there to dry your eyes
There would be nothing you want that I wouldn't give
You would be my queen for as long as you live
I'd build my world around you for everyone to see
I'd show the world how much you mean to me
If you were mine, I'd print your name across the sky
And then I'd tell the world the reason why
I'd tell them that for you, no love is as great as mine
And that for you my love will always shine
If you were mine

Jamaica, A little Bit Of Paradise On Earth

With a beauty so extreme for all the world to see
Jamaica is as close to paradise as can be
How delightful to walk by the sea in its
early morning light
and to sit and stare at its brilliant starry night
It has a beauty of which the half is yet to be seen
A beauty that is befitting a fairy queen
One look at the Island and one can see
What God had meant it to be
He made it with a beauty second to none
Of all the Caribbean island, to me it's the most beautiful
one
Jamaica, a place where people go to live their sorrows
away
A place where beautiful sunlight shines brightly every day
Jamaica, a place where the refreshingly cool sea breeze
relaxes the mind
Jamaica, another place with such beauty which is so hard to
find
Jamaica, with all its beauty and for all it's worth
It's a little bit of paradise on God's green earth

JAMAICA, A NATION SO STRONG

Jamaica, a nation so small and yet so strong
Tell me what is your problem; tell me what is wrong
Why do we fight so much against our brothers?
Why do we see it fit to kill each other
Those of us who are in foreign lands
Refuse to give each other a helping hand
We fight against each other and the world can see
How damaging it is to both you and me
Yet, we refuse to stop and look at ourselves
And to realize that we are hurting no one else
We are a selfish nation, this is sad yet true
and nothing good can come from this for me and you
When are we going to be able to see?
That we need to work together to be truly free?
War, dissension and crimes put us in bondage Continually
But because God is not in our hearts, this we cannot see
I know we are a nation that is small and yet so strong
But with this internal fighting, we won't last long
Here is something of importance that we ought to know
despite the strength that we possess, love is the only way to
go

Jamaica, Land Of The Sunshine Race

Jamaica, to me, you have the sweetest sounding name
Jamaica, land from which our forefathers came
I often dream of you when I'm feeling down
And the thought of you always help me to come around
Jamaica, your shores are so dear to me
And that's how forever they'll always be
I think of you every day
Hoping very soon I'll be coming your way
How I wished I hadn't left you behind
To go to a distant land, what did I hope to find?
I left warmth and friendliness in a land so dear to me
To come to another land where I'm now in misery
How could I have been such a fool, not to realize I was
wrong
And now the feeling I have for home is ever so strong
Jamaica, your shores are home to me
Jamaica, your beauty is all I can see
Jamaica, in my heart, no other land will ever take your
place
'cause you're Jamaica, land of the sunshine race

Man's Best Friend

I stood with my eyes towards the sky
And I ask my God the reason why
Why are sufferings so rampant on this earth?
Is this all that life is worth?
Some will live and some will die
But we watch helplessly while our children cry?
Will you ever intervene? I asked my God
But the answer is in my heart, and it's very sad
He has given us the authority to care for ourselves
But we have become greedy and we care for no one else
There is enough food on this earth to share for everyone
But for his own selfishness, man has dominated man.
Now it's time for everyone to see
The pain, the heartache and the misery
When will this ever end?
When will man be man's best friend?

Method For Success

Dream the dreams you want
Don't ever say you can't
Hold your head up high
Always reach for the sky
Don't stray from your dreams
Though hard it may seem
Don't give up on yourself
Don't depend on anyone else
Your dreams will come true
It can happen for you

MY DREAM GIRL

If I had you in my life, I'd treat you like a queen
Because surely, you're the most beautiful girl I've ever
seen
Your personality is something I've never seen before
And whoever is with you must feel secure
I sat and watched you from across the room
And I was overwhelmed by the smell of your sweet and
delicate perfume
I saw you smile and I tingled at the delightful curve of your
lips
And my heart sank when he touched them with his fingertip
I wanted to scream, to tell him to leave them alone
But how could I, when you're his to own?
He must have been praying all his life for you
And you being here with him was his dream come true
Me, all I can do is watch, hope and pray
That maybe one day
You'll come my way

My Dream Won't Come True

I have so many dreams I would like to see come true
But it seems there is nothing I can do
Sometimes I sit and wonder, why me?
Because heartache and pain are all I can see
I work from day to day
And from hand to mouth is what I get for pay
I see bills in the mail every day
And there is no money with which to pay
I am so confuse, I don't know what to do
All I have are dreams that won't come true
I look around and what do I see?
People who are worse off than me
It's no comfort though, to see the sufferings in the world
today
Could it be the sins of the world for which we pay
I Don't know what to do
All I have are dreams that won't come true
People try to comfort me in many ways
But to me, there is no comfort in what they say
They tell me to continue working and good things will
happen for me
But all I can see is heartache and misery
It seems as if my dreams will never come true
Because to make it happen, there is nothing I can do

My Home, Jamaica

There is a place I always wanted to go
A place where the streams and rivers freely flow
A place where people always want to be
A place with beautiful scenery
A place where the grass is green all year around
A place where there is never any snow on the ground
A place where the sunshine warms the day
A place where little children continuously play
A place where one is free
To enjoy the tranquility of the sea
A place where one can see
Nature's beauty, constantly
A place with a beauty, the half of which has never been
told
A place where the nights are hardly ever cold
A place where one is free to dream
No matter how hard the time seem
This is my place, Jamaica, so beautiful to behold
A land whose true beauty is yet to be unfold.

<u>My Sweetheart</u>
I don't know where I'd be
If I hadn't met this woman who is so special to me
She has that smile which is so incredibly sweet
And that was the first thing that swept me off my feet
I remembered looking at her as if I were transfixed
And all I wanted to do was to kiss those beautiful lips
What caught my attention too, were those beautiful eyes
They had me staring, gaping, completely mesmerized
She has the softest voice I have ever heard
I would try to describe it if only I could find the words
As she approached me, I found my knees becoming weak
She softly said "Hi" I tried to answer but couldn't speak
And then she touched my hand
And an emotion swept through me, only I could understand
She gave me the greatest present I could ever want in life
When I asked her, she said, "yes, I'll be your wife."
Since then she has given me the most beautiful child
One I'll treasure for a long while
I can't help but feel how lucky I have been
To be the husband of the sweetest woman I have ever seen
To me, she is the queen of all mates
One who I'll always love and will always appreciate

GOD'S MOST BEAUTIFUL CREATIONS

How can any man say his dream has come true?
When he has never met someone as beautiful as you
You're a dream made into reality
And I believe you were made especially for me
Your beauty is such a sight to see
And just one look at you mesmerizes me
I can't wait to hold you in my arms
And to experience the magic of your charms
You're everything a man wants in life
And I hope to make you one day my wife
I can't help looking at your picture every day
And I wonder if it could talk, what it would say
You're a very beautiful woman, I'm sure you've been told
And every time I see you, I want to lose control
I want to hold you and to make you mine
But it seems as if it's not possible, why is life so unkind
Just to talk to you makes my heart races with anticipation
And I thank God for you, one of his most beautiful
creations

Our Flag Of Green, Black and gold

Spring, summer, winter or falls
In Jamaica, they make no difference at all
It's just the sun that shines to show the way
So each morning you wake up to a bright, new day
A day that is filled with dreams and hopes
And makes you feel with the anxieties of life, you can cope
Jamaica, land of the beautiful and the bold
Is there any more secret of you that's left to be told
Jamaica, sometimes when there is nothing for me to do
I sit and dream constantly of you
When I think of how cruel winter can be
I think mainly of your sanctuary
A place where it's always welcome and warm
A place where the sunshine always displays its charm
Jamaica, a refuge from the heartache and cold
And represented by our flag of green black and gold

I'LL ALWAYS THINK OF YOU

As time passes, I try to understand
Why you left me for another man
I did everything to make you stay
But still you up and went away
I wasn't the most romantic man in the world
But one thing I know, you were my only girl
I was always there for you
Doing whatever you wanted me to
Still another man came and stole your heart
And I was left shattered and completely torn apart
I thought I was doing everything that's good
But obviously I wasn't doing what I should
You needed love; I gave it to you
But you went away, breaking my heart in two
Whatever you wanted, you could have asked
For you, I'd do even the most monotonous task
I was always willing to go that extra mile
It warmed my heart, Oh! that delightful smile
Now all I can do, is think of you
Imagine, another man holding you as I use to
It saddens me; I've lost you for good
Anything I could do to win you back, I would
Just try to reminisce on what we've been through
And in the meantime, I'll always think of you

A Mother's Cry

Oh lazy child, can't you see?
The pain and distress you're causing me
I have to work hard so that you can eat
Yet you're too proud to remove these shoes
from my tired feet
I sweat and toil to make ends meet
So that I can keep you off the street
But all you do is sit and eat
With the coffee table as cushion for your feet
You never make the bed you sleep in at nights
And you turn on but never turn off the lights
You sleep constantly and think that that is cool
And you are always complaining whenever
you're to go to school
You don't know the significance of an education
And you are much too lazy to understand
That it was just because I was as lazy as you
Why I am now suffering as much as I do

Jamaica, A little Bit Of Paradise On Earth
With a beauty so extreme for all the world to see
Jamaica is as close to paradise as can be
How delightful to walk by the sea in its
early morning light
and to sit and stare at its brilliant starry night
It has a beauty of which the half is yet to be seen
A beauty that is befitting a fairy queen
One look at the Island and one can see
What God had meant it to be
He made it with a beauty second to none
Of all the Caribbean island, to me it's the most beautiful
one
Jamaica, a place where people go to live their sorrows
away
A place where beautiful sunlight shines brightly every day
Jamaica, a place where the refreshingly cool sea breeze
relaxes the mind
Jamaica, another place with such beauty which is so hard to
find
Jamaica, with all its beauty and for all it's worth
It's a little bit of paradise on God's green earth

WE APPRECIATE YOU

You came into our lives and you showed us the way
And for this we are thankful each and every day
We were just kids doing the things we do
But you took us and mould us, and now our dreams have
come true
Because of you, we were made to see the light from an
early age
And as we got older, for us, this sets the stage
You are the best thing to ever happen for us, and this is true
And for that, we veraciously respect you
It's because of you why we're where we are today
And we feel we are obligated to you in every way
We are very grateful for the things for us that you do
And for that we truly and sincerely appreciate you
We are honestly grateful to you, Mrs. Daphne Scott

JEHOVAH, LOVER AND KEEPER OF MY SOUL

The day will come when I will see
The grace and glory that God has in store for me
I will no longer be afraid of what I cannot see
Because He is my God and he has given me the victory
Stress and heartaches will be things of the past
Because my God has shown me the way at last
I will no longer have to search for that which is mine
Because my God is the creator and controller of time
He will not allow me to go astray
And in His path of righteousness I will always stay
He will not allow me in front of my enemies to break
He will give me strength and my hand He will take
He will never allow me to travel this tiring world alone
He will guide me and protect me as His own
He will never allow my feet to be bruised by the earth
He will take me and make me see to Him what I'm worth
My praises and prayers to Him I will forever bring
And my songs of joy and happiness to him I will always
sing
Jehovah is the lover and keeper of my soul
And to serve Him for the rest of my life is my ultimate goal

THE SPOILED CHILD

She had never worked a day in her life
She believed that one day she would become a rich man's wife
Her hands were soft and tender, her eyes innocent and blue
Never one day envisioning the stress and heartache she would now be going through
Her mother had waited on her like a waitress waiting on a guest.
Always doing things for her, filling all her requests
She was never taught what the real world was about
Her mother had thought that if she pampered her, love her then she could shut it out
Her mother did everything for her that was to be done
Never one day teaching her what it was to be a real woman
She was made to believe that the world was a bed of roses and more
Now she has to face life and the real score
She had never given anyone anything before
Her mother had given her everything she had wanted and more
To her the word 'No' was unknown
She had never asked for anything and was ever turned down
She had thought that her mother had loved her more than anything else in the world
And she was really proud to be called 'a Mama's girl
Now she was beginning to see
The world is not what she had envisioned it to be
Her mother is gone and now she is all alone
And now she must face this cruel world on her own.

I Love You Sincerely

Yesterday, I saw the tears in your eyes
But I just couldn't understand why
You said you are happy here with me
But his memories always bring you misery?
You can't seem to get him off your mind
And since lately, you have been crying all the time
It doesn't appear as if I am any comfort to you
God knows I have tried but I don't know what to do
Our love life is not what it was before
And I'm beginning to think you don't love me anymore
You said the memories of him will never hurt you again
But what is this I'm seeing? Is it not pain?
He is with another woman and I'm sure you know
So why do you keep loving him so?
You're no longer on his mind, I'm sure
'cause where you're concerned, he has closed that door
he no longer wants you in his life
'cause he has gone and made another woman his wife
now all I want is for you to be happy with me
'cause I do love you sincerely

I REMEMBER

I sit and watched another day go by
And I found that I still want to cry
I still remember sitting here watching you
And there was nothing I could do
I remember your constant sufferings and your pains
And you calling out my name over and over again
I remember you looking at me with tears in your eyes
And asking the question, why
Why did it have to happen to me?
Why was I afflicted so severely?
You had made a pledge to stay with me forever
And now that you're gone, we're no longer together
I remember sitting beside your bed day after day
And to comfort you, there was nothing I could say
I remember watching your body rocking with coughs
And how painful it was when I couldn't see your laughs
I watched you as your whole body deteriorates
And asked myself, was this to be your fate?
You had given so much to life
But you didn't live long enough to be my wife
We spent a short time together before you became ill
And I remember watching you, feeding on those pills
But they didn't do a thing to help you
If anything, it was more pain that they put you through
When you died, I drank my sorrows away
And to join you one day, is for all that I pray
I will always remember that terrible day
The day fate took you away

Loving You Is All That Matters

Presently loving you is all that matters to me
Yesterday what we had in the past is history
Once in the past we couldn't get along
Everything we did was wrong
I often wondered how is it we said we love each other
When all we did was fight like sister and brother
We just couldn't see eye to eye
And I often wondered why
For us there was such a bright future together
But presently we just couldn't battle that stormy weather
Every time the wind blows, we sank further into the sea
And there was no one there to help either you or me
We were sinking and needed help fast
Struggling, not knowing how long we would last
At times I felt as if I didn't want to be touched by you
And I know you felt the same way too
We knew we loved each other, but what was wrong?
Maybe what we felt for each other wasn't strong
Now with help of God, we have learned how to love
Now our blessings are flowing freely from above
Now what I feel for you is true
And now I can sincerely say "I love you"
Now our love has truly set us free
And I can say with sincerity
Loving you is all that matters to me

A PRISONER'S PLEA

Here where I'm living is sheer hell
So many things happening, half of which I can't tell
I had so many dreams, which just shattered in front of me
Now loneliness and darkness are all that I see
I was happy and had a good life when I was free
But I was foolish; drugs took a hold of me
Now I'm looking at a world, which was once mine
A world I will never again find
I know you're out there in someone else's arms
And getting what is rightfully yours, a man's charms
When I had you, I ignored you all the time
Looking somewhere else, and not at what was mine
Now my world is so terrible without you
And there is absolutely nothing I can do
In my world I get up every day and have a bite to eat
And then I go back to being on my feet
There are so many of us in here, it's a crime
All of us paying for our mistakes, doing our times
I was weak, but I just wouldn't listen to you
When you said my friends were bad, I said it wasn't true
They brought drugs into my life
And for that I ignored even you, my wife
And now I can't stop hearing your voice
Constantly telling me, I had made the wrong choice
I had made the choice to stay with my friends
Not knowing it would lead to my untimely end
Tell me that there is a place for me in your heart
And maybe it will be easier for me to make a new start
I'm here hoping you'll forgive me
And save from my miseries

<u>I Still love You</u>
Tears fell from her eyes as she watched him go
Why did he leave, she didn't know
She had been the best wife she could be
And he had promised her eternity
He told her he wouldn't go, no matter what the
circumstance
But now he is leaving without giving her a second chance
She didn't know what changed his mind and made him decide to
go
All she knew was that she loved him so
He was very good to *her* and then *he* just changed
And started doing things that were very strange
He would come in late at nights
And with her he would pick a fight
She was doing the test she could
But for him that just wasn't good
He would accuse her of having an affair
And told her she just didn't care
He said he was doing the best he can
And she was there cheating with another man
She told him it wasn't true
But to convince him there was nothing she could do
Things got from bad to worse
And he changed from a loving husband to one resembling a curse

Heaven Must Be On Holidays

I saw you for the first time, and didn't know what to say
Your beauty shines as brightly as the perfect day
I wanted to come closer, but I couldn't move my feet
My eyes have never behold anyone so sweet
You are the most beautiful girl I have ever seen
No wonder in England they are looking for a queen
Because you're here with me, tantalizing me
Displaying your beauty so perfect for the eyes to see
I was entranced by such a beauty, and couldn't say a thing
All you need to be an angel are two beautiful wings
I know you have been told that you're a very beautiful girl
And one any man would welcome into his world
You smile, and it helps to enhance your beauty
I look at you and an angel is what I see
I wanted to speak, but I couldn't find the words
And suddenly, it was as if my heartbeats could be heard
Heaven must be on holiday why a beauty like you is on
earth
When you were born, the angels rejoiced at your birth
Give me your hands so that I can lift you off the street
You're much too beautiful for the earth to bruise your feet

I'll Be What You Want Me To Be

I'm beginning to think of you again
And the very thought is causing me grave pain
When I was with you, I was the happiest man alive
Now that you're gone, I'm finding it hard to survive
You were everything to me and more
And when I was with you, I felt so secure
But I took you for granted and I couldn't see
That you were slowly, slowly leaving me
I find it hard to sleep at nights because of you
And I toss and turn, not knowing what to do
My friends tell me to be a man and get over you
But it's easier said than done; it's something I cannot do
I wish I had spent more time with you
I wish I had considered the pain you were going through
But happiness made me blind, and I couldn't see
That I was causing you pain and misery
I'm able to see clearly now, and this is true
I love no one else but you
Give me a chance again and you'll see
I'll be just what you want me to be

I'll Be That Perfect Man

Why did I stay away so long?
I guess I didn't understand
That for emotional support, you needed me
But I was like a child and I couldn't see
That what I was doing was wrong
But still it made me feel like a man
I was hanging out with the crowd
And it made me feel very proud
It made me feel as if I were in control
But I didn't know I was being blatantly cold
I ignored you when you called my name
To me it was as if you were playing a game
I acted like I was a free man
When I should have been living up to my obligations
I should have known I was being led astray
I should have listened when you asked me to stay
I couldn't understand the pain you were going through
And I keep on asking myself, what did I do
Now you are gone, the crowd is no longer appealing to me
They are like a constant reminder of my misery
Losing you has caused me to take a stand
And with you again in my life, I'll be the perfect man

<u>I'll Never Hurt You Again</u>
I'm having nightmares over and over again
Regretting that I've caused you so much pain
I wasn't thinking when I did this to you
Now I'm hurting through and through
I know that you're hurting too
Because I've told you many times how much I love you
but when you needed me, I wasn't there
and I know you must be wondering, why is life so unfair
you're my woman and I forget to say
I wish you a happy Mother's day
And even on your birthday, it was if I didn't care
I know you needed me, but I wasn't there
What should I do
To make it up to you?
I know I do not want to get into a fight
And I know sorry doesn't always make it right
But if you give me another chance to ease your pain
I promise I'll never hurt you again

I'M LEFT IN MISERY

It happened again last night
I felt lost when I saw him holding you tight
You had once belonged to me
But I was a fool and I caused you misery
Now you're his to have and to hold
Now he's the man who is in full control
I see you, and I'm reminded of how stupid I've been
And I wish I had my life to live all over again
I sit by myself at times and think of you
And to win you back, there's nothing I wouldn't do
I can't help but to think how happy he must be
Because he has you by his side continually
When you left, I thought everything would be fine
Now I see how stupid I was when you were mine
I took you for granted, and that's true
It seem other things were more important than you
Now those are things I can't bare to see
Because you're no longer here with me
Now loving you is the most important thing to me
Even though I'm now left in misery

My World Is Falling Apart

My world is falling apart without you
I can't help it; I don't know what to do
You walked out of my life as if I didn't exist
With not even as much as one last kiss
You didn't care what you did to me
I became the unhappiest man in history
Every day I asked myself the reason why
But every time I think back, all I can do is cry
I guess I wasn't man enough for you
But you just wouldn't tell me what to do
Every time I look in your eyes, I could see you were sad
But tell me please, was I treating you that bad?
Why didn't you tell me the way you feel?
So I could change my attitude and get real
Then I would have known what to do
To stop this relationship from falling through

OUR GRACIOUS AND LOVING FATHER

Our gracious and loving Father up above
Teach us your wisdom and your love
Help us as we go along each day
And let us be mindful of the things we say
Teach us how to be helpful to our sisters and brothers
And how to be kind and loving to each other
You send your Son who died to show the way
And for this, we're thankful each and every day
We know that without your love, we can't go on
We know that only your love can keep us strong
We are mindful that you're the one who keeps us alive
And we thank you for each day that we survive
Heavenly Father, I know your love is true
Help us to be sincere in whatever we do
Help us to be beacons to those around us
So they'll know in you they can put their trust

THE LOVE OF A LIFETIME

I woke up this morning and I looked at you
And I couldn't believe it was true
You were lying here beside me
Making real my wildest fantasy
I have always dreamt of having you in my life
Where you could be my lover and my wife
At one time I thought it would never come true
But now I'm here lying next to you
I look at you and I see an angel looking back at me
And I thought how lucky can a man be
Is it possible to have everything in life?
Especially a beautiful woman like you who is my wife?
It's so beautiful when you smile
And I like to picture your face in my mind for a while
I wake up in the morning and look at you wondering if this
is real
And I can't describe to you the way I feel
I'm so glad to be your man
So proud to know I'm a part of your plan
You are the best thing to ever happen for me
And it's a beautiful future for us that I see
You are the love of a lifetime
And I'm so glad that you're mine

YOU ARE VERY SPECIAL

You are very special in every way
Even the angels in heaven celebrate your birthday
Your birth compliments the human race
And you inspire everyone who sees your face
Your smile reassures everyone you see
And around you they feel warmth and sincerity
Your presence is the inspiration they seek
It gives them courage whenever they are feeling weak
One will never lose faith when you are around
Because your presence is enough to put them on solid
ground
You are always smiling and is such a pleasing sight to see
When God made you, an angel was what He intended for
you to be
It's a blessing to know someone like you
You're an inspiration to me in whatever you do

I Am The Luckiest Man

I was searching for you but you found me
How we came to be is a mystery
You came out of a dream into my life
You are so charming, sweet, perfect for a wife
I didn't think that dreams do come true
But I am a living proof; I've got you
I am the luckiest man on the face of the earth
I've got love and all it's worth
Looking at you has made me understand
What real love can do to a man
I was a drifter going away from home
now I no longer want to roam
Here with you is the happiest place to be
and I hope it will continue for all eternity

MY FUTURE IN MY PAST

They say you cannot find your future in your past
But when I found you, I found mine at last
You were the woman of my dreams and I didn't know
I was young and stupid and it showed
I went away leaving you behind
To search for a future I would never find
I didn't know my future was with you
I didn't know you were my dream come true
In my search, I couldn't see
That those other women were not meant for me
But still I try to find one who would understand
The type of man that I am
I searched but it was in vain
Because all I could find was heartaches and pain
Then you found me and you were my saving grace
One mention of your name and everything falls into Place
How could I have been so blind that I couldn't see
That you were the only one for me?
And now I feel at peace at last
Because I have found you again, my future in my past

THE LOVE OF A LIFETIME

I woke up this morning and I looked at you
And I couldn't believe it was true
You were lying here beside me
Making real my wildest fantasy
I have always dreamt of having you in my life
Where you could be my lover and my wife
At one time I thought it would never come true
But now I'm here lying next to you
I look at you and I see an angel looking back at me
And I thought how lucky can a man be
Is it possible to have everything in life?
Especially a beautiful woman like you who is my wife?
It's so beautiful when you smile
And I like to picture your face in my mind for a while
I wake up in the morning and look at you wondering if this
is real
And I can't describe to you the way I feel
I'm so glad to be your man
So proud to know I'm a part of your plan
You are the best thing to ever happen for me
And it's a beautiful future for us that I see
You are the love of a lifetime
And I'm so glad that you're mine

TOGETHER FOREVER

If the world were made for only two
Then it would just be for me and you
There's never been two with so much to share
But with us, it was divinely prepared
God puts us here for us to stay
Living together, forever and a day
Each day of our lives, our love will grow
And our feelings for each other will always show
A love like this happens once in a lifetime
And I'm glad that it happens in yours and mines
With all my heart, I do love you
And I know deep inside you feel the same way too

What You Mean To Me

You are everything to me
My world, my life, my dreams, my reality
Without you in my life, I'd be half of a man
You changed my life and made me see I can
Become anything I want to be
And I'll always want you here with me
To share my dreams you have made a reality
I love you with all my heart
And hope that we'll never, ever be apart

What is Your Secret?

Is there a secret to your looking so young?
Whatever it is that keeps you that way must be very strong
Is it that you have found the fountain of youth?
Or is it that the life you live is so pure and is
filled with nothing but the truth?
You never seem to change as far as I can see
What is it that keeps you this way? Is it a secret or a
Mystery?
If the world could know your secret, then it would be a
much more beautiful place
Because everything that is old and ugly would disappear
without leaving behind a trace
I can't help but to admire your smile, your beautiful teeth
Is there anything so lovely, so sweet?
You're always looking so fine, and is such a sight to behold
This must be a secret, because the half has never been told

YOU ARE A GIFT SENT FROM ABOVE

Where have you been all my life?
You're the sweetest thing a man could ever have for a wife
I know you belong to another, and to him you're true
But if I can't have you for myself, what else can I do?
To him you're the complete image of his dream
Is his world as grand as it seems?
He is always walking with his head held high above the
clouds
He is an outstanding picture amongst any crowd
He is always talking about how sweet you are
He said you are 'the crème of the crop' amongst the stars
He told his friends that he has never been so much in love
He said you're a gift sent from God above
He is never been tired of boasting about you
He said without you he wouldn't know what to do
He seems to be the happiest man in the world
But who wouldn't be, if he had you for his girl?

THE TREASURE HE HAS LOST

If the man you had before could see the future
I'm sure he would want to change the past
He would make sure that you were properly nurtured
And that the relationship would last
He would treat you like a queen for the entire world to see
He would take care that he didn't cause you misery
He would make sure that the ground didn't bruise your feet
Because to you, he would be so sweet
He would walk with his head held above the clouds
Because you would make him so proud
He would have been the happiest man around
Because he would have had the most beautiful girl in town
But the future he couldn't see
And to let you go, he did agree
Now I'm sure that every time he sees you pass
He wouldn't mind if he could get back the treasure he had
lost
But now you belong to me
And I'll love and nurture you for the entire world to see
You're the kind of girl any man would want in his life
And the kind he would be please to call his wife
I thank God that the future was something that he couldn't
see
Because then you wouldn't belong to me

YOU ARE MY WORLD

I sat here and reminisced on the say we met
It was the most beautiful day of my life, one I'll never
forget
You came out of a dream into my world
A sweet, sincere, delightful girl
You are everything I ever dreamt about
And in my mind there is no doubt
For me life was going to be good once more
You were the girl of my dream, of this I was sure
You are everything I ever wanted in a girl
And it was as if you were from a different world
You smiled and it brightened your face
And it was as if you were not of the human race
When God created you, an angel was what he had in mind
Because you're the most beautiful woman any man could
ever find
Your voice is as soothing as a violin
And when you speak, it reaches the very heart within
Your face is as bright as the morning star
And it reflects how sweet and delightful you are
I cannot begin to tell you what you mean to me
But the world has eyes and with them it'll see
That you're the best thing to have happened in my life
And I'm proud that I have made you my wife
You're the very picture of love
A gift that was sent from God above

YOU ARE SO SWEET

Words cannot begin to describe how sweet you are
Your very smile is as brilliant as the morning star
Your eyes are so delightfully blue
They reflect the very image of you
Your teeth are so beautiful to behold
It's as if they were made of white gold
I can't help, but to admire your beautiful skin
Is this a reflection of your heart within?
Someone who is as beautiful as you
Has got to have a heart that's just as beautiful too
How else could you be so sweet?

www.ingramcontent.com/pod-product-compliance
Lightning Source LLC
Chambersburg PA
CBHW022343040426
42449CB00006B/701